Praise for *The Yellow Buoy*:

'It is a book full-bodied in its embrace of life, and the presence of the dying or dead underscores the strength of that embrace. Understood as a sustained reflection on the approach of death, *The Yellow Buoy* is the most moving and most satisfying of all Stead's books of poetry.'
– Michael Hulse, *New Zealand Books*

Praise for *South-West of Eden*:

'. . . a work of literature in its own right, revealing the author's mastery of yet another mode, the literary memoir.' – Lawrence Jones, *Otago Daily Times*

'[A] wonderful evocation of his childhood years in an Auckland in some ways barely recognisable today . . . suffused with the honesty, the insights and the narrative skills we have come to expect and hugely enjoy from Stead.'
– Garry Sheeran, *The Independent*

Praise for *Collected Poems*:

'This ancient poetic theme – how to live in order to live beyond life – runs throughout this massive book, unifying the staggering profusion of forms and contents and linguistic registers.' – Justin Clemens, *The Australian*

BY THE SAME AUTHOR

Poetry
Whether the Will is Free
Crossing the Bar
Quesada
Walking Westward
Geographies
Poems of a Decade
Paris
Between
Voices
Straw into Gold
The Right Thing
Dog
The Red Tram
The Black River
Collected Poems 1951–2006
The Yellow Buoy: Poems 2007–2012

Fiction
Smith's Dream
Five for the Symbol (stories)
All Visitors Ashore
The Death of the Body
Sister Hollywood
The End of the Century at the End of the World
The Singing Whakapapa
Villa Vittoria
The Blind Blonde with Candles in her Hair (stories)
Talking about O'Dwyer
The Secret History of Modernism
Mansfield
My Name Was Judas
Risk
The Necessary Angel

Criticism
The New Poetic
In the Glass Case
Pound, Yeats, Eliot and the
Modernist Movement
Answering to the Language
The Writer at Work
Kin of Place: Essays on 20
New Zealand Writers
Book Self: The Reader as Writer
and the Writer as Critic
Shelf Life: Reviews, Replies and Reminiscences

Autobiography
South-West of Eden

Edited
New Zealand Short Stories (2nd series)
Measure for Measure (a casebook)
The Letters and Journals of Katherine Mansfield: A Selection
Collected Stories of Maurice Duggan
Faber Book of Contemporary South Pacific Stories
Werner Forman's New Zealand

C. K. STEAD

THAT DERRIDA WHOM I DERIDED DIED

POEMS 2013–2017

AUCKLAND
UNIVERSITY
PRESS

First published 2018

Auckland University Press
University of Auckland
Private Bag 92019
Auckland 1142
New Zealand
www.press.auckland.ac.nz

© C. K. Stead, 2018

ISBN 978 186940 889 3

A catalogue record for this book is available from
the National Library of New Zealand

This book is copyright. Apart from fair dealing for the purpose of private study,
research, criticism or review, as permitted under the Copyright Act, no part may
be reproduced by any process without prior permission of the publisher.
The moral rights of the author have been asserted.

Book design by Katrina Duncan
Cover design by Greg Simpson

This book was printed on FSC® certified paper

Printed in China through Asia Pacific Offset

Poems in this collection have appeared in the following periodicals, books, and websites:

New Zealand: the International Institute of Modern Letters' *Best New Zealand Poems*, broadsheet: *new new zealand poetry, Courage, Commitment, Comradeship: 75 Years of the Royal New Zealand Navy, Landfall, Manifesto Aotearoa: 101 Political Poems* (ed. Philip Temple & Emma Neale), *New Zealand Books, New Zealand Listener*, my own *Poet Laureate Blog 2015–2017*, Paula Green's *Poetry Shelf, Sport, takahē, Turnbull Library Record, The Spinoff*; UK: *Arete, The Arts of Peace: An Anthology of Poetry* (ed. Adrian Blamires & Peter Robinson), *Five Dials, The Hippocrates Book of the Heart* (ed. Wendy French, Michael Hulse & Donald Singer), *Paula* (poems for Paula Rego), *POEM, The Poetry Review, PN Review, Scottish Review of Books, Stand*, and *The Warwick Review*; U.S.: *Poetry*.

A small selection, with the title *In the mirror, and dancing*, was made to conclude my period as poet laureate and published in 2017 under the aegis of the Alexander Turnbull Library in an edition of eighty-five signed and numbered copies, beautifully designed and printed by Brendan O'Brien and with accompanying drawings by Douglas MacDiarmid.

I am grateful for constant kind attention during my period as laureate from Chris Szekely, chief librarian, and Peter Ireland, at the Alexander Turnbull Library; to the Matahiwi marae for the welcome I and my whanau received there, and to their carver, Jacob Scott, for the tokotoko, prized symbol of my laureateship; and to John and Toby Buck at Te Mata wines for my two years of the excellent laureate's tipple.

Some of these poems formed a group that won the 2014 Sarah Broom Poetry Prize, which commemorates the life and writing of poet Sarah Broom whose funeral is the subject of the poem on p. 29.

I have added notes on some of the poems at the back of the book.

Contents

CARTOONS and CONTEMPORARIES

An Horatian ode to Fleur Adcock at eighty	3
The moon	5
That Derrida whom I derided died	6
Big Ted	7
Code: poetry	8
A pianist and two poets	9
The widow will not be returning	11
Witchy Wellington	13
My contemporaries across the Ditch	14
2013 New Year cartoons	16

AT DOG POINT

Beauty	25
That summer cento sonnet, 1950s	28
Funeral	29
Artie at eighty	30
Eight pleasant pieces	31
Budapest	35
'J'ai perdu beaucoup de gens.'	37
Another Horatian ode	38
Here and there	39
Spring	39
Oriental Bay, 6 a.m.	39
Can you hear it?	39
Vulpi	40
At Dog Point	41
The sun rising, Auckland, August 2017	42
In a Zagreb bookshop	43

DOUBLE MARGINS

In the June rain	47
The year was '69	49
In 'The Memorial Room'	51
Untitled	53
The artists at eighty	54
1. Lucien Freud	54
2. Henri Matisse	55
3. Paula Rego	58
4. J. B. Yeats	59
The poetry of fact	60
Rain	62

LAUREATE – 2015–2017

Three poems for Kay on her birthday 24/12/2016	65
A Birthday	67
Christchurch Word Festival, 2016	68
3 a.m.	68
Seeing I'm here	68
Tenses	69
The Cathedral	69
Avondale	69
Selina	70
Instead	70
Apprehension	70
Good morning	71
'Auckland': the renaming	72
Long-range forecast	73
WW100	74
Duty	74
Mansfield	74
Gallipoli	75
Malone	75
The bayonet	76
The Ministry wants one on	76

The deserter	77
Quiet there!	77
The C.O. at Ypres	78
Sinai?	79
Jack Lee, D.C.M.	79
'We will remember them'	80
Passchendaele	80
The Somme	81

SYLLABICS: PROPRIETIES and IMPROPRIETIES

Really	85
A matter of time	86
14 x 14: Tercets in the spirit of Brecht	87
The angels of science and compassion	89
Sapphics for Tarore	91
A flash in the pan	93
Amsterdam: the movie	95
That Stephen Dedalus will never be a poet	96
By the back door	98
Hospitality	100
Sapphics for Clodia	101
Syllabics for young rooster	102

NOCTURNES

A morning of remembering...	107
I was the one...	108
Father/s	110
Barry	111
Those difficult Russians	113
Unusual obsequies	114
Ten minutes to midnight	115

Notes 117

CARTOONS and CONTEMPORARIES

An Horatian ode to Fleur Adcock at eighty

When I wanted only to sing
    war and hunting
        it was Phoebus warned me
            remember sooner

friends of your youth, especially
    that princess of quiet fire
        from a southern city
            she of the classic lyre

on which she counted lovers
    one perhaps a prince
        one a certain pirate
            too many to remember

until in middle life
    she gave them all away
        denied herself meat
            and tobacco in favour

of her family's fables
    and deftest celebrations
        of the life of things
            with feelers and wings.

All that's fine in Fleur
    I celebrate and sing
        as you commanded Phoebus
            but on my solo string

        and sounding from so far
            gone in an instant –
                and I still wanting
                      war and hunting.

The moon

for Diane

Six decades after I wrote them an old friend
sends back love poems and a letter. 'Beautiful'
she calls them, but the letter makes her lament

the grief she gave. The critic in me cringes
at my sonnets' lugubrious rhyming and
a plangent prose that owes too much to *Gatsby*.

Do I remember the writing? Faintly, yes
but as we recall the dead, or a landscape
of gold and shadows under a lambent moon.

There's a smiling snap-shot too, a smouldering
twenty-year self fond of ballroom dancing
and tennis. In the letter are dark streets

wet with rain, and I'm carrying flowers,
head full of her loving words just whispered
over the 'phone. But at her gate I see

she's with her new suitor, the golfing lawyer
she will one day marry. I retreat, wounded,
noticing now the moon more silver than gold.

Are these relics to be kept? Two aged friends
once long ago in love debate by e-mail,
and in the moon's absence, 'Your archive or mine?'

That Derrida whom I derided died

We are dispossessed of the longed-for presence in the gesture of language by which we attempt to seize it. — JACQUES DERRIDA

Derrida, enemy of plain sense, my enemy too
determined not to be grasped since understanding

was first step on the road to control – how I disliked you
in the years when your flame swept through the Anglophone world

and had it speaking in tongues. Algeria you loved but lived
in abstract France and the beds of its beautiful women

never coming down in favour of this or that because
commitment, too, was a weapon in enemy hands.

America, whom you taught 'Outside the text there's nothing'
loved you, took you to its hot, hard heart. I see you glance

back over your shoulder, handsome face, white hair, keen smile
of the intellect loyal to nothing but itself.

Critical parricide, fastest brain out of the blocks, how
much better you knew your Rousseau than he knew himself!

I see you on the Paris doorstep of Sylviane who bore
your child and whom, unasked, you are visiting in a dream.

You are a ghost now truly, but the ghost of Derrida –
a voice in the halls, a word on the page, *deconstructing*!

Big Ted

Like Willie's fisherman
'cold and passionate as the dawn'
                                    six foot three
broad-shouldered
any woman might say he was
                                    'to die for'
who when he caught a steelhead
                                    released it
always
                    back where it belonged
for the health of the River
which was sacred –
                            perhaps to die?
                                  no matter
he'd caught it,
he put it back.

I remember the grey stones
                    of Hebden Bridge
Brontë country
in drifting rain

and Cambridge 1958
                              in deepest fog
                              or London '65
where Dr Horder said
even the foxes and crows in Regent's Park
                              had read their Ted
and could be heard rehearsing
their terrible lines.

Code: poetry

for Kevin Ireland

What a talent he has for a book launch!
But then, as part of it, I was summoned

quite un-forewarned, to add my blandishments.
So I recalled we'd both been, long ago,

Grammar boys from schools on opposite sides
of the Harbour, soccer players, and how

years afterwards, remembering a game
when someone's leg was broken and the *crack*

horribly echoed – it was then we saw
this must have been a match we both had played

though on opposing sides – and so, we'd say
it has gone on, goes on, these sixty years –

which makes us what? Rivals? Some might think so –
but more important, *playing the same game!*

A pianist and two poets

Famous young, he sold his piano
    at sixty. Now he's been a quarter
    century without feeling
    fingers on keys, or hearing what

once they could do. Living alone
    among trees in a gully he
    walks with a wheeled frame, the local
    shops his once-a-day visit for

supplies and cigs. But this week the
    butcher closed, greengrocer's long gone,
    he has no car. We used to stop
    and talk, always about the past

when you went to England by sea,
    his tours with big orchestras, and
    his fear of Mother. I can still
    remember his Mendelssohn *Songs*

Without Words in Brighton Road
    the day his roof leaked on the Steinway
    and he covered it with a tarp.
    Allen Curnow put that into

a poem. Allen's as dead now
    as an old friend can be which is
    hardly at all. This morning I
    caught sight of the pianist limping

along in the rain, and turned
    the other way – cowardly, not
    ready for one of those meetings
    you know might well be the last.

The widow will not be returning

i.m. Jeny Curnow

The widow across the street
has been taken to live

with her family, and later
perhaps to a hospice.

Last week I was called to
witness her will. Now Rufus

her little dog has gone to
friends in Entrican Ave,

her neat blue Hyundai is parked
unused in the street, and

her pohutukawa
taller by these forty years

are assuming the scarlet
mantle of another

December. 'The end of an
era,' we say to one

another uneasily in
Tohunga Crescent.

In the Bay the tide
insinuates among mangroves

and goes again without a
word – as it did before

Cook, as it did before
Kupe. The blue heron lifts

itself skyward on elegant
wings and nothing's changed

except, it seems, the widow
will not be returning.

Witchy Wellington

A summer southerly
sky grey
the sea a beat-up
and passing Grass Street
I thought 'Intolerable Lauris' –
not so much, or not just, the person
but the name,
the way those words seemed to belong together –
good company, great fun, wordy and witty
but when backs were to the wall and guns blazing
truth was a stranger.

I'd come down from Auckland
in a lassitude of reluctance
but now here it was again
that same old
pricking of the thumbs.

My contemporaries across the Ditch

Drunken Dad holds forth to fearful Mum while little Bruce, not looking, buries his nose in a comic about flying heroes – until Beaver senior, offended by indifference snatches it and hurls it out the window. Little Bruce flies after it, father follows, they land together on the dunny roof and roll to the lawn. That was Manly in the 1930s.

And across the Continent young Randolph Stow, allowed to ride with the drovers, lies in shade after lunch, dozing and dreaming, watching gum leaves quiver in a light breeze, and sleeps. Waking he finds a committee of emus looking down at him, like a conference of doctors confirming the patient is breathing. The boy laughs and they scatter.

Camberwell 1940 little Barry Humphries stares from the top of his scarlet ladder at a wooden iron-roofed house – kids with dirty faces and bloody knees stare back from a yard of chooks and mangy dogs at the rich kid from the next-door brick-and-tile with sprinklered garden. Barry would like to entertain them. Tries to think of a surprising joke.

And then there was Les Murray motherless in the unlined house on the Coolongolook where words could be made to make bark bandages hanging off grey-brown limbs, or a mare's blood-shot stare as she side-stepped, skin flexing off flies in the heat of his vernacular Republic. The Church would be mother – or it would offer him One.

Peter the rock, Porter the carrier, was motherless too, and would turn his back on Brisbane, saying 'To Hell with anyone's vernacular' – a quiet man whose turbulent underlife surged but never broke the surface, and whose ear for music, eye for colour and line, would tell him we were European still, for good and ill – all, and unarguably so.

Last not least the ghost of Ern Malley looks out from the Nolan portrait, who 'prepared quietly for his death' in that single room cared for by his sister Ethel, leaving behind a life's work, *The Darkening Ecliptic*, that would kill and give life to two pedestrian pens, writing 'I am still / The Black swan of trespass on alien waters.'

2013 New Year cartoons

for Michael Laurie

21.1.13
Prince Harry compares
killing Afghans from
an Apache gunship
to computer games –

Playstation for example.
With practised thumbs
and small royal brain
he does it well.

His Dad's delighted –
says he's 'Making
the Nasties keep
their heads down.'

24.1.13
Police in County Kerry
will issue the elderly
licences permitting them
to drink and drive.

'If we shut them up at home'
 says councillor Healy-Rae
'the young will be deprived
of their songs and stories.

'All that wit and wisdom
and Irish lore
will be lost if they can't
be drunk at the wheel.'

28.1.13
After Obama's
second victory
the Republican Party
is unhappy.

He will take away
the guns America needs
to defend itself
against itself.

In Virginia
they want to change
the rules so Romney
would have won.

29.1.13
Speaking to reporters
on Holocaust
Memorial Day
Signor Berlusconi

who has been reading
Mussolini's letters
has a kind word
for Il Duce.

It's true he sent
Jews to Wherever-it-was
but his help to Hitler was
'not entirely conscious'.

31.1.13*ns
Iran has sent
a monkey into space
and brought it back
(this time) alive.

Iran has oil,
Iran has heavy water.
Now Iran has a simian
astronaut-survivor.

And on Iran TV – look
here's a new device
for sawing off the
fingers of thieves.

6.2.13
America's new
Secretary of State
John Kerry
first day in the job

sends a message
congratulating us
on the anniversary
of our Waitangi Treaty.

He thinks we've set
the world an example.
So has he – start
with the easy stuff.

8.2.13
In Leicester
a dig has discovered
a king in a carpark –
his broken skull

and crook-back spine
confirming this is
Shakespeare's
story-book killer

of the boys in the Tower
who lost a kingdom
only for want of
'*A horse, a horse!*'

10.2.13
As much as
twenty-nine percent
of your United Kingdom
beefburger

may have pulled
a Romanian cart,
or run a race
or chased a fox

but don't complain –
it's good protein and free
of detectable feline
or canine traces.

12.2.13
Why am I shocked
his Holiness has
chucked it in?
Shouldn't he have died

like the old Pole
in agonies
of age and office?
What's the job

for Christ's sake?
'*Pain,*' I hector.
'*Pain!* Isn't that
the name of the Game?'

18.2.13
The Duchess of
Cambridge with
her plastic smile
dead eyes and

spindle limbs might
have been designed
by a committee
suggests Hilary

Mantel, whose
body clearly wasn't
but whose novels
might have been.

20.2.13
On 'Kill-list Tuesdays'
the President
signs off the names
of those who are to die

far from Washington,
usually at home.
Ever efficient
the United States

doesn't need to put
a Prince up there
thumb on the button.
They do it by drone.

AT DOG POINT

Beauty

1. Like a bird
   for Kay

Long ago, remember,
when we lived on the beach
at Takapuna, a Texan

teacher of maths bought a
fisherman's dizzy wife for
one thousand pounds – a good

price, equal to one year's
professional salary.
All three – the fisherman,

the Texan maths-man, the
wife – were pleased with
the deal and partied

to celebrate. I recall
the fact more clearly than
the party. Much wine was drunk,

and so, soon, were the drinkers.
There was a moon on the sea
right out to Rangitoto.

You were beautiful, and I
sang, as I could in those days
all the way home – like a bird.

2. Terrible beauty

Yeats prayed his
daughter might be granted
'Beauty', but not

so much of it
she would drive suitors
mad, or herself

in the looking-glass.
Seeing her once
where the river

runs out from the
Lake of Innisfree
I thought she might

well have been
the plainest woman
in all Ireland

who'd lived a long
life with a famous
father's famous

and foolish
petition so patently
not granted.

3. In Genoa

where the B.V.M. is crowned
annually as the city's Queen

Here the Mother of Jesus
is painted often as if
by a sceptic soul who works
in secret from a model

or a sentimentalist
whose vision ratifying
faith's most difficult demand
makes her a pretty Virgin.

Hail holy Queen do you hear
the streets of the city ring
with gratitude and praise for
your promised intercession

while the Ligurian Sea
whose beauty came before yours
and will outlast it teaches
only to trust what is so?

4. The signer

Not singing but signing
with subtle hands and mobile features she makes
something of nothing and a song of silence.

That summer cento sonnet, 1950s

for Robyn Marsack, who will get it

That summer it seemed we wrote only of islands,
sun on sea and on pohutukawa.
War had rumbled off into history.
We were at home now bidding the godwits go.

Always to islanders, we'd grown tired of intoning
danger's what comes over the sea, while meeting
and parting make tremulous the salt-rimmed air.
Who would teach us to stand upright here?

Frank and Allen, Robin, Ron and Rex
rode the North Shore ferries, while Rangitoto
pictured itself sunk in a stone composure.

Even the Golden Weather would have to end
where a small room with large windows disclosed
geraniums wild in the wet and a gannet impacting.

Funeral

Sarah Broom, 1972–2013

How could the oarswoman, tennis player
scholarship girl, the poet of such delicacy and finesse
proprietor of that generous smile
mother of three small children lighting now
each one, a candle in her honour and to
                                        her memory
how could the lover of this tearful husband
who reads the poem in a strong voice in which she is
                          his *Schmetterling*, his butterfly
how could the daughter of these noble parents
he addressing us all, she talking to her grandchildren in our
                            presence but as if we were not here
how could this lovely, surely unquenchable fire
                                          burn out so soon
and the name of God yet be spoken
as if there were reasons, justice, divine and eternal love?

The thrush sings in the thorn-bush,
the day, and the days, go on
nothing understood or able to be explained
except that loss is random, and pain unjust.

Artie at eighty

Undressing for bed alone
he caught on the *Late Show*

'Sad Sack' by Artie Shaw
and his Gramercy Five,

and saw himself naked
in the mirror, dancing.

That night he dreamed
he carried a sealed despatch

to a tyrant who demanded
his name and rank.

'I am Artie' was his answer,
'and a long-time dancer.'

Eight pleasant pieces

for Alan Roddick

1. That we all go together

Yes certainly
I must be one of
an endangered

species. Orange
roughy? Orang-utang?
The golden

oriole or
the white tiger
of Borneo? No.

I am Humankind
endangered by
my own success.

2. Faith

If the Lord were his shepherd
he would not want
in the Valley of the Shadow
protection against wild dogs.
He would be well-shorn
for the Lord's back,
and in due course well-slaughtered
for the Lord's table.

He is not, however,
(or believes he is not)
a sheep.

3. My clerihew in French

Les Baux
c'est beau
mais Beaulieu
c'est mieux.

4. R.S.V.P.

When she you loved once
so briefly the memory is faint,
and he you disliked so long ago
the reasons are forgotten,
invite you, Catullus
to their elderly wedding
in a Roman garden,
what can you wish them
but the best –
what can you offer
but a blessing?

5. Pound sterling

One hundred years ago young Ezra writes
from Kensington to Miss Alice Kenny

of Paeroa telling her he's setting
'the stiffest standard in Europe'. He wants

not 'stuff for magazines' but 'masterworks'.
'Absolute impulse, perfect rendering'

are what he requires. 'It's a tough hurdle'
he knows, but thinks she should 'give it a shot'.

6. Sufficient

In the secret micro-climate magicked by
our heat-pump's outflow, arum lilies flourish
out-sized with ferns and a native orchid
against the wooden fence, and are alone
sufficient. This is the poetry of fact.

7. The human condition

Olive? Yeah she called again this morning,
wanted me to sign a petition about Gaza.

I made a joke. You know the Milton line,
'Eyeless in Gaza at the mill with slaves'?

She asked me what I meant. I wasn't sure.
'Nothing,' I said. 'It was a joke, that's all.'

What can you do? Makes it tough at the net
having to think about the human condition.

Anyway Steve, the court's free this evening.
Fancy a couple of sets while the weather holds?

8. Looking up, looking back

Swimming on my back between the yellow buoys
at dawn, I could discuss with you, my mother
what kinds of cloud, what sea-sounds you might choose
to decorate and grace a grave in the sky.

There are white bouquets edged with pink and scarlet
and stone grey puffs against an infinite blue,
and whispers as of your Swedish father's schooner
wishing you back to romantic latitudes.

Still in my skull there are those indentations
the forceps made pulling me out of you.
You could not breast-feed but you taught me love
and I escaped and did not pay my dues.

Swimming on my back between the yellow buoys
let's talk, not about cloud-scapes, but rather why
your son ran off to learn the world as it was
and tell its stories to an indifferent sky.

Budapest

i
Today
outside what was once
Party Headquarters
a weary summer square
known locally as
'Dogshit Park' remembers
'The Martyrs of '56.'

ii
There are weeds between the tracks
but the yellow tram to the Palace of Arts
where Wagner will be heard
is clean and quick.

iii
Lunch was a strong pâté
of raw onions and chives
with a hint of garlic and mushroom –
delicious with bread rolls and ham
and a small side-bowl
of feta in oil.

iv
These are just shoes, but cast in bronze
and set in concrete
marking the place where Jews were shot
so their bodies fell in the Danube
and were swept away.

v

From the hill at night
in floodlit bridges and castle
and holy places
Budapest re-imagines
the old look of Empire.

'J'ai perdu beaucoup de gens.'

1820: St Helena

Power but not honour lost, he sits
his exile out waiting for Time to turn
in his favour. Melancholy rules but

memory can have its hour. In a moment
of causeless elation he remembers
Joséphine in bed, and Marie Louise

on their first hot night telling him, 'Don't stop.'
He goes over the so-called 'victory'
at Eylau of which he wrote home only

'I have lost a lot of men'; and those long days
when the Russians would not engage, their retreat
drawing him ever into winter and

the random rage of the serfs. He dreams of
Moscow in flames and wakes in a fever.
When his young aide is leaving, he taps his cheek:

'Till the next life, my friend. Come – embrace me.'
On that grim rock under a British flag
in a rough wind he walks with officers

rehearsing the great days, days of glory;
or lies long hours in his bath, nursing
the pain in his side that will be his death.

Another Horatian ode

Peace, great Augustus, can be yours –
    it is only an edict away:
        say 'I will not be Caesar,

'will not honour the poet who sings
    "Sweet and proper it is
        to die for one's country,"

'nor the casuist asking why
    unheard our brothers call us
        to save them from the tyrant.'

Honour instead the Moon
    when she rules in shadow
        unbroken by flame or sword,

the city untouched by fire,
    the streets not running with blood,
        the forum where music sounds.

Celebrate the olive and the grape,
    the fish in the net, the lovers
        yawning at daybreak,

and the dreaming poet
    who calls upon you, Augustus,
        to be greater than you were.

Here and there

Spring

Kowhai knows
and tells by tolling
yellow bells.

Oriental Bay, 6 a.m.

Wellington windless
lacking the whip and the lash
can be lovely.

Back to the wall
feet in the flood
asleep on its elbows
it waits to be woken.

Can you hear it?

In England
there is much to be
learned from / said for
summer rain
in a green foxy wood
drumming on the roof of leaves.

Vulpi

Through an iron fence
of the locked park
he sees the three
fleet shadows
purposeful
scholars of silence
mariners of midnight
under an icy moon.

At Dog Point

After a day of frost and sunshine
in the valley of winter vineyards and winding streams
that teach the far brown hills by definition
and the farther mountains by peaks and caps of snow
Dog Point at 4 a.m.
showed me the night of another world
created by gods and peopled by their children
each one distinct, a point of brilliant light
each family a constellation
and needing all together
a name to match and affirm their magnitude –
'the Heavens' for example or 'the canopy of the stars'.

There is a dream of love
so far from the avidities of lust
and dramas of fidelity and possession
it is like that southern sky at night
burned across by a single shooting star.

The sun rising, Auckland, August 2017

> '*The dead writers are remote from us because we know so much more than they did.*' *Precisely, and they are that which we know.*
> —T. S. ELIOT

John Donne
struggling for a rhyme
to round up and tie off the tight form of a poem
he will call 'The sun rising'
does not know that a reader
400 years hence and half a round world away
on his morning walk is struggling to remember
the same concluding rhyme.

After erratic weeks
of late winter wind and the rains of early spring
the plum trees have exploded in whitest blossom
distracting the walker from his memorial task.

Addressing the poet as Dr Donne
he explains the contingencies
of elderly recollection.
The Doctor looks up, half-listens
and dismisses the phantom,
finding at just that moment
the couplet they both require:
'Shine here to us, and thou art everywhere;
This bed thy centre is, these walls thy sphere.'

In a Zagreb bookshop

'When your armies are defeated,
your leaders dead or in exile,
your enemy in the Chancellery
and his militia on your streets,
it is then, my friend, your language
becomes a power.

'It is the impregnable gate
and the house of your pride.

'That is why if I should say
"He is a writer"
you will receive respect.
But if I should tell them
"He is a poet"
respect becomes honour.

'Poets are the guardians of the language.
Pray you have them.
Pray you never need them.'

DOUBLE MARGINS

In the June rain

Peter Porter is dead, Peter Porter is . . .
        Splashing around green Cleveland Square
      (gardeners planting in the June rain)
I say the words over
          remembering two decades ago
climbing the five flights to his flat
side by side with Anthony Thwaite
         each going faster, a little faster,
Peter waiting at the top, laughing at us
because we were competing . . .

             And earlier, 1975
  under bluegums at Macquarie
  arguing about Les Murray's
  'vernacular republic'
           and the poems of Pope.

        'Peter the Rock' I called him,
     'Porter the Carrier' – and sometimes
(acknowledging a facility, a felicity)
'Prêt à Porter'
       the runaway Australian who made
London his home
Italy his university.

                    Three years ago I listened
in the Spiegeltent at Edinburgh.
He had come out of hospital to read
and went back there to die –

                                  the poet Porter
fondly remembered
in the June rain.

London, 2013

The year was '69

for Sam Sampson

Reading your poem
                         and re-reading my reading
I remembered the bar
               Colin painted for Maurice
                         in the studio
         among trees
     below the house
above the inlet
at Arapito Road
                       with a text that said
because there is a constant flow of light
we are born
into a pure land –
and the words had to curve with the bend of the bar
and the flounder net down there among mangroves
                      pulled round by the tide.

The year was top-and-tail / it was soixante-neuf
    when Tricky talked to Neil and Buzz on the moon
        and Dave smoked pipe dreams in Ponsonby
and Colin painted
                'All mortals are like grass'
and Maurice made the most of one summer's dolphin
              and with Barbara made a beginning
and with Beverley an end.

The vomitty green and velvet blue of the bar
I remember
and the one word 'Ahipara'

                              painted in black
book-jackets pinned to the wall at irregular angles
                    and the inner Manukau stillness
                                sliced by cicadas.

                          Vietnam was always there
we breathed it and lived it and fought it in our sleep
                              and despite the moon
                      making America great again
and Strawberry Fields supposed to go on forever
it would not go away
                          My Lai stuck in the throat
              and Agent Orange and the Tet Offensive
and could not be dislodged.

No end in sight and yet it would have to end
         and the air of the age was full of the soothe of sex
      the iambs Dave tried to hide and his secret rhymes
scent of the dope that would drain
                                    his Keatsy brain
and Hanly's garden
and Wedde's golden girl.

                         It was the year of the Rooster
                                  year of your birth
with its beards and hair and students' unwashed dishes
              when songs had words you could remember
                        and tunes you couldn't forget
when for all the self-destructs and all their tears
                                 the world could seem
still an enormous room
                    still an extravagant promise and
an unfolding dream.

In 'The Memorial Room'

Janet Frame's posthumous novel

    This blue sky
                      blue sea
           she seems to have seen
    neither
                 attuned only
    to her own
    inner
               culture of complaint

    blind to orange roofs
    and ochre walls
               and the transparencies
                      of a sea
    with so many
    memories

              deaf to the gulls
    which when the wind is up
                cry all night
    and the daylong
    twitter of swifts

      neglected when none will help
      put upon when help is offered

        is this ingratitude
                              or only
                     the solipsist's
sad and solo cantata?

Menton, June 2014

Untitled

A winter swim can be
                a voluntary
        almost-orchidectomy.

Three hundred metres
          off the beach at
            Kohimarama
penis shrinks
testicles retreat indoors
            the old man's
a boy again
watching a liner
          round North Head
     and triangular Rangitoto
crowd the horizon.

On your back now
    see how cloud-fleeces float
        in a Disney blue
      and the lost moon's
pale ghost
haunts deep space.

How clear this chill makes it
           the Platonic
beau idéal
marriage of true minds
         the perfect match
            but alas
scoreless.

The artists at eighty

1. Lucien Freud: the mirror

           Sensitive youth
      confident middle-age
elderly arrogance
        all gone dissolved
into the ugliness
of eighty years
       but mirror-reversed
in his favourite Georgian
over-mantel
wearing nothing
        but unlaced boots
palette in one hand
    palette-knife in the other
          faithful only
to his talent
          true always
to what it sees.

2. Henri Matisse: the models

With Henriette

                    Her energy,
his colour, and sometimes
           no more than a single
unbroken line,
made *La Danse*.

                Or she could be
                   Odalisque
languid,
dark hair, dreaming eyes
                    à la mode
d'un monde
                    tout en fleur
tout en couleur.

After Henriette

    When his children told him
(echoing Paris)
in his new work
was nothing new
    he told them it was precisely
himself at this moment and
               to be continued.

The 1940s – Nice

        Now while the world
tore itself apart he painted
          that phoenix palm
beyond the window, and
nudes as never before.

'I don't touch them,'
      he told his friend Rouveyre.
        'Like Delacroix I've attained
perhaps
contented impotence.'

The Chapel at Vence

     At eighty he's tasked to design
a Catholic chapel.
Atheists are shocked.
          'Why not?' he asks.
      'My only religion is the work.
I celebrate myself.'

'Why not a brothel,' Picasso suggests.
'Nobody asked,' he replies.

With Lydia

      All his life he'd measured
          the worth of a work
by its cost in effort.

Only at the last came this
       'certainty of execution'
            costing
    him next-to-nothing,
receiving his all.

3. Paula Rego

   Her Camden workplace is
a cavern of dolls
stuffed animals
     platforms and ladders
      up to her white
nightmares –
   the man whose hands are
turtles
the prince who was a pig
    the dogs that were dogs
     or maybe gods
and a doll that is a cut-down
Amy Winehouse . . .

      She is story-teller
magician and witch
    who shows it as it was
in paint
and pastel action
not letting you forget
     the grimmest Goyas
downstairs at the Prado
as if she might have been
     his dark daughter
who taught herself laughter.

4. J. B. Yeats: the never finished self-portrait

       This last was to be
         his Masterpiece
go out with a bang
    nothing less than greatness
so he gave it
     nothing less than his best
day after day, year after
        eight long years
alone and cold in New York
living on hand-outs
   writing reports to the woman
('Today I re-did the hand')
         Rosa in London
he said he should have married
whose portrait of long ago
     was truly the Masterwork.

The poetry of fact

                        On board Apollo 13
              on their slingshot return
from the mission which failed to land them on
the moon
oxygen diminishing
CO_2 increasing
                    temperature dropping and
                          batteries failing
they had to get a precise
angle of re-entry.

Too steep and they would burn
too fine they would bounce off
earth's envelope of air
and away into space for ever.

                   Prayer would not help
though by now the whole world
              the President
                the Pope
        the people in Times Square
were praying.

                    To do the job
they needed Physics
                and after Physics
Maths

                        just numbers you could say
                             or an illustration
                    of how hard the hard facts can be
how exacting
and necessary
and beautiful
                        when you get them right.

Rain

Now iron roofs and gutters
           come into their own
        as drummers, timpanists
calling on Noah & Sons
and praying that the god of
rainbows
remember his promise.

The big drain chokes on its swallow
              and throws up,
the tide-out bay
has the sheen and reflect of fullness,
     and everywhere, even in a lull
there's the rustle still,
the whisper and whistle of water.

        Green is never so green
as the colour of after-rain
         when birds set in,
      and Tamaki-makau-rau
wahine with one thousand lovers
shakes east and westward
over two harbours
        and an isthmus of cones
           her cloak
         of feathered cloud.

LAUREATE - 2015-2017

Three poems for Kay on her birthday 24/12/2016

1. Photo: the poet is anxious on the marae

Here I am, laureate on the marae
at Matahiwi flanked by mythical creatures
carved in wood and painted in green
and over our heads
the hook that Maui used to catch
the land under our feet.

And here is Kay, and here
our children are, and mokopuna
and poet friends, Chris and Greg and Paula.

Tokotoko in my left hand
I'm reciting a poem or making a speech
as if it's the end of the world and no hereafter,
only these green carved monsters of Matahiwi
and a waiata that must surely bring me
to the end of a line, a last full-stop.

2. A dream of lost daughters

Maurice told me his daughter
was lost in the post.
He looked so like King Lear
I thought of Cordelia and said
'Sorry for your loss.'

'No need,' he said and I remembered
he was the one who'd died
and how at his funeral we wept
singing 'The carnival is over'.
I told him my daughter
had gone to Antarctica.
It didn't mean she was dead –
just lost in the frost.

3. The laureate's last . . .

His last
was not least
nor yet his best
but shaped for a shoe
his size
and like his sighs
not to last.

A Birthday

The N.Z. Navy turns 75

We were all sailors once –
Tangata whenua, tangata tiriti
We came by sea

Cradled, or at work in the rigging,
Becalmed or storm-tossed or
Backs bent to the paddles,
That was our passage –
There was no other.

So it was written in our blood
That the path South was only
Over the ocean's face.

Blue water and a moon at the masthead,
Language of sky and cloud,
These and the flying spray remember
What we have been,
Where we have gone.

Born of a navy
Of a naval nation
And of Polynesia,
Today, together
We salute our own.

Christchurch Word Festival, 2016

3 a.m.

From the 9th floor
of the Hotel Rendezvous
I watch a taxi
dawdle down a wide wet street
between two wastelands.

A wind drags at a flag:
the flag resists
the wind persists . . .

Cold out there!

Seeing I'm here

Four opposing mirrors
in the otherwise empty
hotel lift
show me myself
in unwelcome detail,
a very old man.

I had no idea!

I want to apologise and say
it's not for long.

Tenses

Here are the buildings
cordoned off /
        boarded up
that have a **were**
and perhaps a **will be**
but no **is**, no **are.**

The Cathedral

I come around a corner
and there it is –
the broken heart of a city.

Avondale

Shops and houses
even the debris
a whole suburb
swept away
done and dusted
leaving streets and grass and trees
and the river winding by
as if to say nothing
is what happened –
as if to say
nothing, it was
nothing.

Selina

The beautiful Pasifika giant
sniffed and said
'What's that you're wearing?'
and then
'Verbena!'

So there we were
sniffing –
the old poet-man
and the cool-cat rapper
with hair like black fire.

Instead

And then rain stopped
sky cleared
sun came out
and the sensitive nor-west afternoon
that collapsed in Curnow
was revived in Stead.

Apprehension

In the dark
of the 15th floor
Bill Manhire woke
thinking the building
had turned over in sleep
and groaned
    or ground its teeth.

A little boat of a moon
was sailing west
over the flat landscape
guided by a single star.

Good morning

And now looking east
from the 9th floor
I see the sun truly is
that boring old
    ball of bullshit fire
in all its gold glory.

'Auckland': the renaming

Now that we know
he was only another
imperial duffer,
a Caesar's bumbling sidesman
and journeyman of Empire –
couldn't we quietly
wipe him from the record
and give back the name
tangata whenua first
accorded her –
Tamaki-makau-rau
our clement isthmus
between two harbours
and two oceans,
hub of the South Seas
loved by too many?

Long-range forecast

for Paula Green at 60

August and still winter
but the purple iris is out
under the vine
and suddenly every branch and twig
of the plum is pricked with blossom.

This is an oath sworn by the season
hand on heart.
It's in the sky too between showers.
The days are longer
and the wet green lawn is sprinkled
with a white hail of daisies.

Today from the blue bridge
that crosses to Tamaki Drive
I saw three dogfish
          in what we used to call 'formation'
coming in with the tide.
The sun lay over the sea
out past Devonport, far out into the Gulf.

'Soon,' it whispered, 'soon'
and you knew it could be trusted.

WW100

Duty

One hundred years ago
we were at war
and the Ministry wants from Catullus
commemorations.

'Why me?' he protests.
'I can give you only
"Brother, hail and farewell!"

For "How right and proper it is
to die for one's country"
you need a civil servant –

Horace for example.'

Mansfield

Remember Katherine's
Beauchamp brother
the one she called Bogey
killed teaching bombing
in Plugstreet Wood
on the Belgian border
that set her writing
memorials and laments.

'Blown to bits' she told a friend.
'My darling little brother –
    blown to bits.'

Gallipoli

Paddy was the doctor's dog
and died of shrapnel wounds
in the same good cause
and for the same good reason
the soldiers died.

What was it again?

Malone

There were wildflowers
among the shimmering
    fly-blown dead
and he wrote about them.

He thought his men should fear him
and wanted glory.

Yes they took Chunuk Bair
and lost it
and would be remembered for that.

But he hadn't foreseen the love
   he would feel for them
and that nothing would be worth so much
as this brotherhood in death.

The bayonet

Practice had been
           on a sack-full of straw
in out and on
           stomping on the face.

But this was a man
and the blade stuck
           deep in his rib-cage
dragging me forward
           as he fell.

I had to plant a boot on his chest
to yank it free.
           His eyes were open
but glazing over
           like a fish
just pulled from the sea.

'Sorry' I said, and *on*
           not stopping
to stomp on the face.

The Ministry wants one on

the contribution of women
so Catullus records
that Clodia gave white feathers
to cowards
and lived to shed
           tears for them.

'Feathers and tears'
 says Catullus.

'Feathers and tears.'

The deserter

Last words of the one
who had to die at dawn
in an orchard in France:
'Are you there, padre?' –
and the padre was there
though not close enough
to hold his hand.

    The last things
he likely saw
were the apples
        red-ripe
in green grass
and the five-man squad
rifles ready.

Quiet there!

That noisy boy
in No Man's Land
whose actions rhymed
crying and dying –
the Sergeant wanted to shoot him
to shut him up
but couldn't risk the shot.

The lad fell silent
at 2 a.m.

    By noon
we could smell him and soon
could hear between bomb blasts
the flies
       that sang in his ears.

The C.O. at Ypres

            Starved
  hung on a willow pole
    by wrists and ankles
in freezing snow
   the hours passed in pain
    and passed beyond it
for Archie Baxter
         his will
        resolute
valiant
hardly human
    who would not fight
   nor serve in any way –

a sort of scarecrow,
a kind of Christ.

Sinai?

The Ministry
     suggests for subject
'the forgotten war
         in Sinai'
which Catullus
alas
    can
not
quite
     remember.

Jack Lee, D.C.M.

It was the detonations
                            and worse
the spaces between
                         kept him awake
when weariness put his mates to sleep.

Death would be better than this
         but at night in No Man's Land
                   repairing the wire
he dived to avoid it until
a shell shredded his arm.

Then a coolness
came upon him
                and he did everything
                   to save the life
which in battle
he'd been ready to squander.

    Gallantry was the word they used
for the daring, the sheer dash
            of his exploits under fire.
He called it madness.

'We will remember them'

My brother is a number
and so is my cousin
    and my cousin's cousin
and so now am I
one of a number.

On brass and in marble
    they will remember us
    and will call us
'the glorious dead'.

Passchendaele

was the endless rain
        the ever and always mud
the dying and the dead.

                It was
sleeping upright on the fire-step
because the trench was flooded
        and at daybreak
walking into the fire
        of our own shells
  that were to clear a path ahead
but falling short;

and then the snipers
                        picking us off
as we ducked between shell-holes

    brains blasted, lungs blistered . . .
      but more, worse

             it was the endless rain
the ever and always mud
the dying and the dead
and the pain.

The Somme

Mud and blood
so much of it
but don't forget
(Catullus insists)
the boozing and singing,
the brotherhood,
and those easeful epiphanies
in the brothels of Bruges.

Tell the Ministry
it was a man's war.
To men most of the pride,
to men all of the shame,
and to Owen Vincent Freeman
a grave in Armentières
and a bronze plaque saying
'He died for Freedom and Honour.'

SYLLABICS: PROPRIETIES and IMPROPRIETIES

Really

In London theatres I've been taken for
playwright Michael Frayn. 'There he is. Go on,
tell him how much we're enjoying his play.'

Once, at Hay-on-Wye, I told a group
including the man himself, of this mistake.
Everyone looked at him. He said nothing,

his face unsmiling, a mask suggesting
'Like *you*? *Me*? Fuck off – who would think that?'
I moved away, cursing the weak impulse

to plug a talk-gap with whatever comes
unthinkingly to mind. Just at the door
a woman stopped me. 'Mr *Frayn*,' she exclaimed.

On my desk a postcard of his portrait
shows we're not twins, it's true, but you can see
at a glance how the mistake might be made.

Why don't we invite him to New Zealand
where someone in the street might stop him with
'Mr *Stead*, I do admire your novels,'

or even, 'Karl, you cock.' But then suppose
he was recognised only as Frayn. No –
we're worlds apart really. Let's keep it so.

A matter of time

When I was young it was C. P. Snow averred
anyone who did not know the Second Law
of Thermodynamics was uneducated.

'Two Cultures' was his bag and what he wanted
was scientists reading poems, Arts chaps Maths
in lunch breaks and on the beaches in summer.

So I learned it and was briefly, you could say,
'educated' until, like so much else,
the discriminating brain discarded it.

But there is a shadow of it lingers still –
something about the universe winding down,
and how we can't drive history in reverse

because of entropy, which means the world's end
is only, you could say, *a matter of time!*
The comprehending stars which know this Law

are sad about it and don't burn so brightly.
The birds too are affected in their singing,
less jubilant in spring; and even my cat

dislikes it when I mention Thermodynamics,
its Second Law, and twin-cultured C. P. Snow
who thought this something a clever cat should know.

14 x 14: Tercets in the spirit of Brecht

In my dream the eight-
tonne golden Buddha
was melted down

and ounce by ounce
distributed among
Bangkok's poorest.

The Vatican was
selling off its art
for refugees;

vows of poverty were
reaffirmed, those
of chastity

annulled. Reason was
breaking all bounds
as the homeless were

offered shelter in
the tombs of kings. Saudi
girls drove

taxis, their princes
manned oil-rigs in hard
hats and the Haj

was discontinued.
Israel's offers to
assist Iran

were politely
declined; Ireland
embraced the condom with

abortion on demand
and Americans
gave up guns.

Prayer went out
of fashion and the vast
legions of the dead

pleased to be forgotten
were left at peace. As
dawn broke came

news the Queen had
been allotted a good
half-acre on

her Sandringham
estate and urged
to Dig for Victory.

The angels of science and compassion

Women (he tells himself) have had to get used to
male doctors since forever, so why should men not
accept the reverse? *'Absolutely!'* And no buts?

Only that he's 'getting on', and that he hasn't
needed, not until now . . . and that it demands
something new – you could call it a discipline . . .

So when for example she's fragrantly close,
her stethoscope near to his sternum, listening
for that faint *intra-cardiac shunt* in the beat

signalling *patent foramen ovali*, there's
the impulse to give the top of her blonde head
an affectionate peck. That has to be resisted.

And then there was the time when, recovering
(both, it seemed) from the more than slight frisson
of her rubber-gloved lubricated finger

in his anus checking the prostate, he had to deal
with the thought of joking, 'My turn now?' No, no –
surely she would not have laughed. How could she?

And now, today, her last patient for the morning
when they talked as friends might, and she told him
her husband was away, wasn't it only –

not propriety, not fidelity, but the sense
of age and age's follies prevented him
saying, as once he might have, 'How about lunch?'

How splendid they are, these angels of science
and compassion, in whose hands, but not in whose arms,
he must expect, sooner than later, to make an end.

Sapphics for Tarore

died 19 October 1836 at Wairere Falls

They killed her with a small axe then took her heart
and the top of her head. This was the custom,
utu on first killed, and the girl Tarore
        was certainly first –

the only one in fact, the rest escaping
into the bush – except the catechist Flatt
protected by the Church's tapu. So they
        took his clothes and tent,

left him his horse to ride back naked, in tears
to the Tauranga Mission. From her they took
the flax kete on a thong about her neck
        in which she carried

St Luke's Gospel translated into Maori.
Later, it was said, the Arawa chief was
converted by this text, and the tribe with him
        and sued to make peace.

On her grave the inscription reads 'Tarore,
whose St Luke Gospel brought peace among the tribes
of Aotearoa.' Now if there was war
        it would be only

with Pakeha, and their kupapa Maori.
Flatt's grave cannot be found though it's thought he lies
somewhere in the Te Aroha cemetery
        close to the racecourse,

while the young woman the Maori Queen ordained
should be remembered, lies here, an honoured ghost
of tribal war. So history writes itself, and
      sometimes revises.

A flash in the pan

The occasionally
    mad writer who last
        called five years

ago to warn me my
    world would soon
        be ending, and

whose exalted
    paranoia was
        the subject of

his last book, phones
    now to confide he
        thinks he has just

ten years left in
    which to summon
        up the power of

his Irish genes and to
    achieve something
        on the scale

of James Joyce or
    G. B. Shaw. He seems
        deaf and hears my

attempts at small talk
    as unwarranted
        interruptions

  becoming more
    excited while he
      warms towards the

true greatness that
    beckons. After
      twenty-five minutes

when I say I'm
    sorry but I have
      to go, I hear

his voice turn
    hard and threatening.
      Am I to die, should I

bolt the door?
    But no, I suspect
      this will mean only

another of his
    killer reviews
      like the one of

my *Collected Poems*
    where he declared
      all my books

to have failed since
    the long-ago first –
      a success but

one which time has
    proved was only a
      flash in the pan.

Amsterdam: the movie

Tucked among books, look, a long-ago letter
long ago lost, thanks me for poems – for one
especially in which she's named. I remember

saying goodbye at Regensburg. We'd eaten
a meal of meatballs and sauerkraut with beer
while snow-flakes drifted and the Danube swirled

through ancient arches. She'd said she was pregnant,
her husband away, and those keen eyes told me
she wanted what I wanted, and quite as much.

In a movie your hero doesn't wonder
'What about Amsterdam / my hotel / my lecture?'
And 'Could today's ticket be used tomorrow?'

I asked myself those questions. Sadly we kissed
and I boarded the train. The letter tells me
the baby was a girl, her name, Eva.

I should have stayed a day, found us a finer
place to dine, bought her a silver knife to slice
open the marvellous letters I might write.

Eva must be thirty now. I imagine
her saying goodbye on a station platform
to the ghost of a poet. I say to him, 'Friend,

fuck Amsterdam and don't think of home, just think
of Eva, and pleasure. Tell yourself virtue
will starve you of stories, and life's a movie.'

That Stephen Dedalus will never be a poet

*for Hayden Murphy in Edinburgh, Massimo Bacigalupo
in Genoa, and Declan Meade in Dublin*

Father Conmee, unable to find a coin
small enough to give the one-legged sailor,
reflects if the man had served his God as his King
he would not now be on the streets, a beggar –

but blesses him. Ned Lambert's remembering
how Kildare set fire to the Cathedral and said
'I'm sorry, but I swear to God I did it
because I thought the Archbishop was inside.'

And aren't they in and out of bookshops spending
their pennies well? – Bloom buying one for Molly,
Sweets of Sin – and Stephen telling his sister
the primer she's bought to teach her French is good.

Distracted at the place where Emmet was hanged
Tom Kernan is too late to doff his chapeau
to the Viceroy's carriage. In the coffee shop
Buck Mulligan wearing his primrose waistcoat

is telling Haines, 'That's Parnell's brother playing
chess in the corner.' Stephen, he says, has been
unbalanced by the Church's visions of hell
and will never be a poet, but he'll write

a book, 'perhaps in ten years' – (*and so he will!*)
And there's young Dignam bearing the porksteaks home
wondering do the boys know his father's dead,
hoping drunk Pa made a sober confession

that will see him safely into Purgatory.
Now here comes Blazes Boylan, straw hat and suit
of indigo serge as, smilingly Vice-Regal,
the cavalcade of carriages trundles by.

Auckland, Bloomsday 2013

By the back door

C. K. Stead has always suffered from a surfeit of lucidity — DAMIEN WILKINS
Clarity is poetry — JOHN RUSKIN

After a dozen
novels, some good
runs, translations,

a movie, and
prizes won, it
came to Catullus

while reading one
by Elizabeth
Bowen, that *this*,

not what he'd been
doing, was what
the *real* novel was –

not clear but
opaque – and *delay!*
spinning it out with

something always
unclear, unresolved.
It's Auden says

the novelist must
'become the whole of
boredom' while

poets 'dash forward
like hussars', and it
was as if that dash

all along had been
his undeclared
intent. A wrong

path? Maybe, yet he
looked back on tales
that had been worth

telling, the bigger
picture no lyric
could command,

the cut and thrust
of talk too – and *scenes*,
out-reaching mere

prose. So yes, it might
be time to stop, but
he was still

Catullus and would
keep his own secret,
sneaking out

by the back door
with no announcement –
and no regrets.

Hospitality

My mordant friend told me the story of
the woman he loved in youth in Cambridge
who had, he said, 'a hospitable cunt'.

That was the obstacle – hospitable
to him, but to others too, and he was
in love. I met her once in middle years

still beautiful, and with a voice to charm
and command. The slightest incisor gap
was that single imperfection they say

the gods impose on those they favour.
Later again she had the gap repaired
giving herself new beauty in old age.

Hospitable still, the cunt? I can't say.
My friend married of course, but carried
that flame for her, and was unforgiving.

Sapphics for Clodia

It was as if Catullus travelled the world
with his cell-phone switched on – didn't understand
how it worked, or comprehend what 'flight mode' meant
    or even have it.

Clodia, in love, told him weeping she had bought
new underwear for their adventure. He found
a pheasant dead on the roadway and plucked her
    one of its feathers

to write him a poem. Leaving her (she recalls)
he stamped on the rain-soaked lawn to show her how
it sighed underfoot – as if he didn't know
    her soul was grieving.

All this you understand is 'for example'.
It was long ago before the days when phones
were kept in pockets. He was himself the one
    'switched on', 'charged up'

not knowing there was an 'off', only rarely
conscious of fault. 'Predator' would you say, or
'natural man'? Either way he loved too many
    and was loved too well.

Syllabics for young roosters

It was London's burning
tower made me recall while

doing dishes that my friend
Les Parker's real first names

were Grenfell Bertram Louis.
He came from Seddon Tech

to MAGS and attached
himself to me maybe because

he detected 'Welcome' under
the Grammar School bluff.

His mother called him Gren
he called himself Les, only

I was allowed to know
the secret full-blown horror –

which made us allies until
the sixth form when he stole

my girlfriend – lithe and
lovely and too clever for Les –

Jean Lamont. Later hearing
they'd married I wondered

what became of them, where
they'd gone – enquired among friends

hunted through phone books – but
now, my hands in the sink

after decades / transitions
of faces and places

I had the fullness of that
name, the whole caboodle

and took it to the highest
authority not God

of course but Google. Up
it came at once on a grave

in Allambe Memorial Park
Queensland 'Grenfell Bertram

Louis Parker' (in full in
bronze – had he grown to like

it?) 'Dearly loved, sadly missed' –
but loved and missed by whom?

It didn't say, and where was
Jean? Had there been no one to

recall his black curls, how
he bounced about in the ring,

his jokes on his racer
pretending (or was it real)

brain damage? But maybe
I had it all – everything

a poem needed or a
friend could ask about Les

boxer and biker now
eternal on a plaque in

a cemetery-park on the
Nerang-Broadbeach highway

beside the bright Clubhouse
of the Roosters Junior League.

NOCTURNES

A morning of remembering...

A morning of remembering merged into
an afternoon of drink and forgetting
sweeping into the gutters the black soot
drifting over that southern city
that had never been mine. I had bought you
a cotton kimono – beautiful, yes, but knowing
it should have been the silk, and even
in a dream this was something that had to be
a failure. And Death was everywhere.

I was the one . . .

I was the one who believed in poetry –
that it could capture the gull in flight
                        and the opening flower
                        and in the blink of an eye
a knock on the door of death.

I believed with Shakespeare
                there was a trick that unlocked
                        the mystery of
the named stars.

                I remembered the ever green
ever golden
oleanders
                        were not to be taken
                        or eaten
and especially that at the gate
                of every social success
Shame built his willow cabin.

How darkly we discoursed in dreams
on childhood
and the long fall of *la Rue du*
                    Cardinal Lémoine
            towards the now that was Paris –

and how my friend's imaginary friend
                  composer of his own fame
would stop the taxi
outside the church of
Saint-Étienne-du-Mont
             and copy bell-notes he might use
to end a work he was planning,

and drive on
scattering leaves like letters
                and blessings like bombs.

Father/s

And I saw in my
dream *Herald*
headlines: *Elderly*

*writer Frank
Sargeson weeps on
Takapuna Beach*

while above the
sound of waves
I heard my Dad saying

'I think I was
conscious that the
debt of happiness

had to be paid
but the lad lived
always beyond me.'

Barry

Later, lying on the lawn of the big house
someone asked could we remove our jackets.
No one had taken charge
         we were young officers
    and I took mine off.

   And then (or earlier)
         we were in the battle zone
taking cover behind parked cars
             post-boxes, phone booths
     and in abandoned trams
when my friend took one full in the chest
    and went down without a word.
         'Way to go', I thought
and imagined the sniper reporting 'I got one'
      and being doubted
   but I could have attested to it
the perfect shot.

And then the shelling and the strafing began.

Later I wrote a report (I was good at that)
and I remembered lying out on the lawn
      of the big house
   that was called 'Mandalay'
      in the hot sun
   and Barry asking about our jackets
       and I removing mine
and Ian saying 'In the enemy army
       you could be shot for that.'

>   The battle zone was not always a city
>   sometimes it was jungle
>   where our first foes
>   were mosquitoes
>   who took our blood
>   like bees, Barry joked
>   taking pollen
>   from the full flower of our youth.

Those difficult Russians

I am travelling on the northern line
    in a freight wagon (open-sided)
        with a baby grand
      and an adjustable stool,
watching the greenscape go by
    and hawks drift over;
        and near Whangarei
          in sight of a sea
blue and calm and stretching away from me
I am playing Rachmaninoff
        Scriabin
those Russians I found in childhood
            so difficult.

I am heading for the Bay of Islands
      and that calm inlet
where the *Bay Belle* will land Allen and Jeny
        over from Paihia,
and where my mother on her honeymoon
        watched from the hotel balcony
    my father swimming

            playing with such ease
better than ever she heard me play before
          Rachmaninoff
      Scriabin
those difficult Russians.

Unusual obsequies

for Nicholas Tarling who died swimming

In Shallowsleep, that life-of-the-mind that comes
at 3 or 4 a.m., hearing big rain

beat on the roof and spill from broken gutter
to concrete path, and quoting to myself

(faultlessly) a sonnet of a single sentence
and great complexity by Willie Yeats,

I promised I would call that comic-strip
tradesman I had named, just to amuse you,

Gutterfix. It was the day we'd buried Nick,
historian, daily dipper, opera aficionado

with song and stories of his gloomy wit.
'Come to our aid, great Gutterfix' I sang

in my opera voice, and laughed, and seemed to fall
a moment after into a dream of drains.

Ten minutes to midnight

She was, she tells me
the one without a partner
until I came
with a bottle of bubbly and two plastic cups
and a small box of rose petals.

'You realise my age?' I ask
(uncertain what it is).
'Of course,' she says.
'This was half a century ago.'

So we danced and danced
until just before midnight
when I walked out
into the Bavarian dark.
'I've never forgiven you,' she says.
'Where did you go? Where have you been?'

And here I am again
dinner jacket, bow tie
with the bottle, the plastic cups,
the rose petals
happy as we dance
in the town square,
surprised we move so freely
so gracefully over the cobbles
under a Munich moon
and a town hall clock telling me
it is ten to midnight.

Notes

p. 6   'That Derrida whom I derided died': The Derrida quotation is the same one that torments the character Helen White in my recent novel, *The Necessary Angel*, and the poem's implications seem to accord with views expressed by Louise Simon-Jackson, editing an edition of Flaubert's *L'Éducation Sentimentale* in the same novel. These ideas, thoughts, literary attitudes, are not unconnected with my poem 'By the back door' on p. 98 (see note below).

p. 9   'A pianist and two poets': The pianist was David Galbraith, who died 26 December 2013.

p. 26   'Terrible beauty': Two Yeats references here: the refrain from 'Easter 1916', 'A terrible beauty is born' and 'A prayer for my Daughter' – 'May she be granted beauty . . .' etc.

p. 28   'That summer cento sonnet, 1950s': A cento is a composition made up of quotations and references. Those that make up this sonnet are from work by Allen Curnow, Frank Sargeson, Charles Brasch, Robin Hyde and Bruce Mason, all of whom lived for a time on (or, in the case of Brasch, visited and wrote about) Auckland's North Shore.

p. 33   'The human condition': I wanted the poem to make it clear that I sympathised with Olive and not with the speaker, but it refused, reminding me of Keats's injunction against poems which have 'a palpable design upon us', and insisted on neutrality.

p. 41   'At Dog Point': A vineyard in Marlborough where I was housed during the Marlborough Festival 2017.

p. 47   'In the June rain': I last read with Peter Porter in the Spiegeltent at the Edinburgh Festival, 22 August 2009, where we made a trio with Hugo Williams. He died in April the following year.

p. 49   'The year was '69': The personae are Colin McCahon, Maurice Shadbolt, President Richard Nixon ('Tricky Dick'), astronauts Neil Armstrong and Buzz Aldrin, poet Dave Mitchell, Shadbolt partners or wives Barbara Magner and Beverley Bergen, painter Pat Hanly and poet Ian Wedde. The poem is addressed to poet Sam Sampson, who was born in 1969 and lives in Titirangi. His poem recalling the bar Colin painted for Maurice triggered these memories.

p. 51   'In "The Memorial Room"': My review of this posthumously published novel by Janet Frame appears in my selection of essays, *Shelf Life: Reviews, Replies and Reminiscences* (2016) with the title 'Janet bites the Hand . . .'

p. 58 'Paula Rego': I contributed this poem to a collection designed to celebrate (but never to mention) the fact that Dame Paula was eighty. It was put together by her partner and principal male model Anthony Rudolf. For my eightieth she gave me a signed lithograph from her Prince Pig series of 2006.

p. 67 'A Birthday': This was my first commission as laureate – to please write a poem commemorating seventy-five years since the Royal New Zealand Navy came into existence with an identity separate from the Royal Navy of which it had previously been part. A page had been prepared for it in the commemorative publication, *Courage, Commitment, Comradeship*, but they were going to press next day and wanted my poem by morning. I grumbled that this was impossible, but did my best overnight and they liked what they got and used it. I haven't revised it or tried to improve it in any way: it's not very good but it stands as an example of the laureate doing his duty!

p. 68 'Christchurch Word Festival, 2016': This was the first time I had seen the city since the big earthquakes.

p. 74 'WW100': The title of this sequence is from the section of the Department of Internal Affairs in charge of all commemorations of the centenary of New Zealand's involvement in World War I, 1914–18. It was suggested that I, as laureate, might write something appropriate, and some suggestions were made, including something on 'the role of women in the war', something about the 'forgotten campaign' in Sinai, 'the introduction of conscription', 'the impact on families', and so on. No pressure was put on me; there was no sense of an obligation – simply an opportunity if I felt inclined. I did have a sense that currently fashionable pressures were being exerted within the DIA, and my first inclination was to push back. However, this small sequence was the result and it was published on the WW100 website with the heading POET LAUREATE'S REPONSE TO THE FIRST WORLD WAR CENTENARY. By way of explanation, or excuse, I wrote:

> These poems were written at a suggestion from WW100 that as poet laureate I might contribute to the commemoration of a century passing since New Zealand's involvement in World War I. My response was to take the persona of Catullus (one I have used often before in my poetry) unwilling to celebrate death in battle as Horace does ('Dulce et decorum est pro patria mori') but able to honour and bid farewell to his brother ('frater ave atque vale') with typical Catullan irony, noting the lack of 'glory', the sadness, ugliness and waste of war, while acknowledging that it sometimes brought out strength, courage and mateship. I finished the sequence with a word for my great uncle, 12/3015 Private Owen Vincent Freeman, First Batallion Auckland Infantry Regiment, killed in action, the Somme, 16 May 1916 and buried in the Bonjean Military Cemetery, Armentières, France.

These small poems were the best I could do. So much about that war is unpalatable it's difficult to see how any of it can be commemorated without some elements of irony, horror and disgust.

p. 89 'The angels of science and compassion': Across the fourth and fifth stanzas the doctor is listening for a 'shunt' in the heartbeat which can sometimes be detected in cases where the hole between the left and right upper chambers of the heart has not entirely closed after birth. This not unusual hole (known technically as patent foramen ovale) is often associated with migraine headaches. I suffer migraines intermittently and patent foramen ovale has been detected. To the doctor it is only a matter of curiosity whether she can detect the characteristic 'shunt'. She was not, by the way, my present GP who probably believes rectal examinations for prostate should be left to the specialist.

p. 91 'Sapphics for Tarore': Sapphic metre employs a four-line stanza form, the first three lines eleven syllables, the final line five, used by the legendary Greek woman poet of Lesbos, Sappho, and by the Roman poet Horace. The Church Missionary Society catechist here, John Flatt, was my great-great-grandfather on my mother's side. The killing of Tarore figures significantly in my novel *The Singing Whakapapa*.

p. 98 'By the back door': Frank Sargeson loved to quote the Auden sonnet, 'The Novelist', which represents poets as dashing hussars and novelists as toilers. The Damien Wilkins quotation comes from an interesting review in *New Zealand Books,* 'The self-loathing of a Stead novel', in which he suggests my novels hate themselves for not being poems. 'To poetry's angel, prose is the necessary donkey.' I wrote this half-serious farewell to fiction certainly before I had written my novel *The Necessary Angel*, and possibly even before the previous one, *Risk*.

p. 100 'Hospitality': The 'mordant friend' was a Scottish-born London literary editor, now deceased, who is represented (though with a shift backwards in time) in my novel *The Secret History of Modernism*, as Marx MacLaren.

p. 101 'Sapphics for Clodia': Catullus is a persona I have used often over the years to distance my real self from my poet self. The Roman Catullus wrote many poems about his involvement with a woman he called Lesbia who is thought to have been in reality Clodia, wife of Metellus. In my Catullus poems (sometimes close to translations and sometimes removed some distance from the originals) I have used the real name, Clodia, to avoid the confusion of Lesbia with lesbian. See the note above, re: p. 91, on the origin of, and syllabic count for, the form described as Sapphics.

p. 102 'Syllabics for young roosters': The London disaster that had prompted the memory of my friend's name here was the Grenfell Tower fire of June 2017.

By an extraordinary co-incidence I had done the Google search described here, and had written a first draft of this poem, when a letter came from a Helen Parker in Sydney. She had seen what I had written about her parents, Jean Lamont and Les Parker, in my memoir *South-West of Eden*. She told me they had had three children, that Les had had drinking and gambling problems, and that they had divorced. Both were now dead. Les's peculiar behaviour on a bike is partly described in *South-West of Eden* (where his concussion in the boxing ring is recounted, and his mother's anxieties about it) and again in the character of Frano Panapa in my novel *Talking about O'Dwyer*. Thinking back on all this I wonder now whether Les's 'blackouts', which at the time I suspected might be fake, were in fact real, and whether the problems in later life described by his daughter had been a consequence of brain damage in youth.

p. 114 'Unusual obsequies': Professor Nicholas Tarling was a colleague at the University of Auckland, professor of history and expert in classical music and opera. The Yeats 'sonnet of a single sentence' was the one that begins 'While I, from that reed-throated whisperer'.